Dr Joseph Bell

The Original Sherlock Holmes

Robert Hume

Dr Joseph Bell
The Original Sherlock Holmes

Illustrated by Cheryl Ives

Stone
Publishing
House

First published in 2005
Stone Publishing House
17 Stone House
North Foreland Road
Broadstairs
Kent CT10 3NT

ISBN: 0-9549909-0-0

Typest in 13pt Bembo by Troubador Publishing Ltd, Leicester, UK
Printed in Great Britain by
The Cromwell Press Ltd, Trowbridge, Wilts

Dr Joseph Bell

The Original Sherlock Holmes

Chapter 1

The door of the lecture hall at the Edinburgh Medical School opened and a tall figure with sharp, eagle-like features entered, glanced around the room and made his way towards the centre. As he walked he looked as though he had difficulty controlling his legs, as though there was something wrong with them.

The room was packed with students, not just local-born lads from the city but those from wealthy families overseas – from Portugal, the West Indies, Brazil, even Australia – who had come to study at the most famous medical school in the world. All were men, for no women were allowed to study at the medical school then. Sitting nervously on their hard wooden benches around the platform, the students were expecting a *long* lecture. The lecturers always taught at length. The students would write *long* assignments and would sit *long* examinations.

But this lecturer was different. For a start, he had a sense of humour. It was not compulsory for students to attend lectures but they would flock to hear this man.

As he reached the reading stand he began to sway back and forth, curling his long fingers over its top. He cleared his throat ready to speak. The man who stood before them was barely forty years old yet his hair was already white. He drew himself up to his full height. His thumbs dug into the lapels of his long frock-coat. His piercing grey eyes stared at the students. As they watched, he leaned forwards, towards the edge of the platform, so close that when he spoke every student thought he was speaking to them individually.

'Gentlemen, this morning I shall demonstrate my Method to you.'

There was not a sound in the room. As the

students waited, he produced from his pocket a glass test tube and held it up towards them. Those nearest the front would have been able to see that it was filled with an amber-coloured liquid, not unlike wee!

'This, gentlemen, contains a most powerful drug,' he said. 'It is *extremely* bitter to the taste. I wish to conduct an experiment, to see exactly how many of you have developed the powers of observation that God granted you.'

He paused and looked around the room. There was a gleam in his eyes.

'I want you all to taste it!'

The students looked horrified.

'Yes, I'm sure you are wondering why you have to do this and why you can't just analyze the liquid chemically. But I want you to *taste* it.'

The students looked at one another and grimaced. They thought they were being asked to sample something disgusting. They knew their teacher could be eccentric but this was ridiculous!

The lecturer stepped forward. He fixed his eyes on

the students in the front row.

'Why do you shrink back? I assure you that I would never dream of asking anything of my students that I wouldn't be prepared to do myself. Therefore I will first taste it before passing it among you.'

He positioned himself under the gas lamp, close to the operating table itself. The liquid in the test tube gleamed more than ever now.

The students stared back in some confusion.

Suddenly, with a dramatic gesture, he pulled the stopper from the test tube and waved it under his nose – once, twice, three times. Then, tilting it slightly, he proceeded to dip one of his long, slender fingers into the liquid. All eyes were focused on him as he lifted his finger out of the tube. They could see the dreadful mixture trickling down the side of his hand. There was absolute silence as he raised a finger to his mouth and licked it. What would happen? The students waited with baited breath.

The mixture must certainly have tasted vile because his features were contorted, his eagle-beak nose more prominent than ever.

But he recovered quickly:

'Now, gentlemen, I want you to do the same.'

The students looked alarmed as he handed the tube to the first unfortunate victim in the front row, a local Edinburgh lad, who hesitated for a moment but reluctantly did as he had been asked. Immediately, he pulled a face and quickly passed it on to his neighbour.

Each student in turn tasted the bitter liquid. Some tried to get rid of the taste by dragging their tongues across their sleeves.

At last, when there was no more liquid left, the test tube was handed back to the lecturer. As he stared out at the faces of his students, he looked disappointed:

'Gentlemen, gentlemen. I am disheartened to find that not one of you – not a single one – has developed his powers of observation. You know how much I have emphasized these before. I call it my Method.'

He paused and looked around the room. 'If you had really paid attention to what I was doing you would have seen that although I placed my index finger in that awful brew, it was in fact not that finger which found its way into my mouth, but my middle finger. You will never make great detectives if you are so unobservant.'

A chorus of groans went up from the students. They felt they had been tricked.

Suddenly their tormentor began to laugh. 'Gentleman, I have made my point. It is these little details, these trifles, that you must look out for. They can be crucial in any diagnosis, whether medical or criminal.'

Among the students staring back at him he saw the face of the first student to sample the liquid, a young man he had noticed before – a student of promise.

'Let us now put my Method to the test again. This time, I need an assistant: Conan Doyle! I have chosen you today! We have some more interesting experiments to carry out.'

The young man in the front row stood up and said

'Thank you, sir.' But he looked rather apprehensive.

The other students looked relieved. They did not know what their lecturer, Dr Joseph Bell, had in mind for their friend, Arthur Conan Doyle, and certainly, little could any of them have realized that the relationship between these two men would become so important. For it was Dr Bell, with his scalpel-sharp mind who provided the inspiration for perhaps the most famous fictional detective of all time – Sherlock Holmes, with his characteristic pipe, deerstalker hat and magnifying glass. Without Dr Bell there would have been no Sherlock Holmes!

Chapter 2

Joseph Bell was born in 1837, the same year Queen Victoria came to the throne. The Bell family was one of the oldest Scottish families, possessed a coat of arms and could trace back its history to the Middle Ages. Joseph was the eldest of nine children – six boys and three girls – which might seem a lot to us today but was not unusual in the nineteenth century when some of the children were expected to die young. The earliest Bells, hundreds of years before Joseph was born, had taken part in heroic raids over the English border; but Joseph's father, grandfather and great-grandfather had all been Edinburgh surgeons. The family had a good reputation and lived in a fashionable part of the city.

Religion in Scotland was always taken seriously and Joseph's father was anxious to see that his son received a thorough religious education. He sent Joseph to a small private school nearby when he was six years old, and when he reached ten his father paid to enrol him at the famous Edinburgh Academy. The curriculum here was very advanced for the time. The day began with Latin and Greek, and was followed by French and German. And that was all before break! Afterwards came Scripture, Geography and History. In fact, before the day was out Joseph might well have been taught English Literature, Philosophy, Book-keeping, Mathematics, Geometry, and even some Architectural and Engineering Drawing! He was a bright student and, to the delight of his family, won first prize in Scripture, and second prize in Greek History and Mathematics.

But despite his success at the Academy, Joseph was not too complimentary about his teachers. In those days it was not against the law for teachers to hit and beat pupils, and Mr Gloag, his Maths teacher, was deadly with the tawse, a leather strap with two thongs at one end. During lessons pupils used slates to write on instead of exercise books. The trouble was that it was very easy to make a screeching sound on the slate with your chalk. If you made a screech and Gloag heard it you were in serious trouble. Even for a tiny screech he would give you a strap on the hand (a 'palmy'); and if the chalk was sharp and made a really loud screech he would whack your bottom.

But Joseph did not spend all his time at the Academy studying. He loved to play hailes, a team game played with a long-handled bat with a scoop like a spoon at one end. It often got rough, the ball was 'slogged', and players were 'mauled' and 'charged' at.

The young Joseph took the awards he received at school in his stride. His main thoughts kept turning to the subject that had interested recent generations of his family – medicine. Experiments and investigations fascinated him. He had to go on to study medicine.

The question was which medical school should he

attend? Joseph Bell was not the kind of young man to be hurried into choosing somewhere. Being by nature observant and methodical, he decided to examine all the possibilities. First he packed a bag and travelled to Holland, to the University of Leyden; but the teaching there was all boring lectures which did not suit him at all, and he returned home. Here he quizzed his father's medical colleagues about the schools of medicine in Paris and London and weighed up the pros and cons of each. After all that, he surprised everyone by deciding to apply to the Edinburgh Medical School which was just half an hour's walk away from where he lived! And he never regretted the decision. It was fast becoming the greatest medical school in Europe. Only a few years before, one of the lecturers, Dr James Young Simpson, had helped revolutionize surgery when he introduced chloroform as an anaesthetic to relieve pain during operations.

Over the next few years Joseph was to make great progress in his medical studies. The professors introduced him to the techniques used by the famous

Greek doctor Hippocrates – the Father of Medicine – when he had examined his patients during the fourth century B.C. It was called the Clinical Method of Observation and Diagnosis. Joseph was taught how to observe patients closely in the Infirmary, watch out for little signs of illness and ask them about their symptoms. By using case studies of other patients who had also experienced these symptoms he would reach a diagnosis, know what course the illness could take and treat it so that the patient would get better. Such attention to detail Bell practised throughout his life, both in medicine and when trying to solve crimes.

* * *

While Joseph was developing his skills of observation and deduction, Arthur Conan Doyle, the fresh-faced student who was to taste the vile liquid in Joseph Bell's test tube, was about to be born in a very different part of Edinburgh.

Arthur's childhood was unsettled. His father drank

heavily and was unable to keep down a job. To support the family his mother was forced to take in lodgers. One of these lodgers, a doctor, encouraged Arthur's interest in medicine, and he enrolled to study medicine at Edinburgh University where he soon developed into an enthusiastic student.

Of all his university teachers, it was Dr Joseph Bell who made the deepest impact on him. They say that you never forget a good teacher, and Dr Bell was truly unforgettable with his beak-like nose, his shock of white hair and his strange manner of walking. But it was Dr Bell's powers of observation and deduction that impressed young Doyle the most.

One morning, as Bell was just about to start his lecture and the students were all attentive in their seats, a woman entered the lecture hall with a small child. Bell had never met her before, nor knew anything about her. He greeted her politely and she replied with 'good morning.'

'What sort of crossing did you have from Burntisland?' he asked her in a flash.

'It was guid,' she answered.

'And did you have a good walk up Inverleith Row?'

'Yes.'

'And what did you do with your other child?' The woman looked taken aback.

'Why, I left him with my sister in Leith.'

'Are you still working at the linoleum factory?'

'Yes, I am,' she laughed.

The students were stunned! How on earth did Dr Bell know all this? Bell turned towards them: 'Well, gentlemen, when she said good morning I noticed her Fife accent. The nearest town in Fife is Burntisland. Did you notice the red clay on the soles of her shoes? The only such clay within twenty miles of Edinburgh is the Botanical Gardens. Inverleith Row borders the gardens and is her nearest way here from Leith. Did you observe the coat she carried over her arm? It is too big for the child who is with her; therefore, she set out from home with two children. Finally, she has a rash on the fingers of her right hand. This is often found amongst the workers at the linoleum factory at Burntisland.'

As he began to understand each link in the chain of reasoning, Conan Doyle nodded slowly. It was all so obvious really. He opened his notebook and began to write down the conversation – more for a keepsake than anything else. Or so he thought at that time.

Another day, Bell was interrupted by a patient walking straight into the room while he was in the middle of giving a lecture. Bell stopped in mid-flow: 'Look!' he exclaimed. 'You can see that this gentleman has been a soldier in a Highland Regiment, and that, being short, he was probably a bandsman! Look at the swagger in his walk. Only a piper walks like that!' He turned to the patient. 'Am I right?'

'No, you're not!' the man replied smartly. 'I am a shoemaker! I have never been in the Army in my life.'

Bell could not believe he had made a mistake, and he asked two of his clerks to take the man to one side and remove his shirt. Here they found that under his left breast was a little blue 'D' branded on his skin. So he was a deserter! No wonder he refused to admit he had been in the Army! Bell grinned with satisfaction.

But some of his students wondered. Could it all have been a set-up to impress them?

* * *

Although Arthur Conan Doyle was a keen student, he was not able to devote his whole time to his studies. Always worried about how hard up his family was, he tried to squeeze each year's study into just six months, which left half the year free to work as a medical assistant. The jobs were never very demanding and he found plenty of time to read and write – even selling the odd adventure story to magazines.

Doyle impressed Bell. He was not the ablest student he ever had (he later admitted that he was 'more of a 60% man') but his enthusiasm and potential for learning was in a class of its own. By the end of Doyle's second year at the University, Bell had plucked him from the lecture hall benches to help him as his outpatients' clerk.

This gave Doyle the chance to observe Bell's razor-sharp deductions at first hand, as when he said to one patient: 'I see you're suffering from drink. You even carry a flask in the inside breast pocket of your coat.' To another he said: 'Well, my man, I can see by your fingers that you play some musical instrument for your livelihood, but it is a rather curious one.' The man afterwards confessed that he earned a few pennies by blowing 'Rule Britannia' on a coffee pot!

Bell urged Doyle to take notice of all the little details about his patients. He explained to him how physiognomy (a person's physical features) would help him deduce a patient's nationality; how accent would reveal the district where he lived; and how the condition of his hands and the way he walked would give a clue about his job. Some of the students wondered why any of this mattered. Of course it matters, Bell explained. 'If a patient can see that with just one glance you can tell so much about him, you have won his trust. He will have complete faith in your ability to diagnose his condition and to treat it.'

Chapter 3

Each morning, Bell and Doyle made their way through the streets of Edinburgh towards the University Medical School. Each came from a different direction. Bell lived with his wife Edith and their three children – Jean, Benjamin and Cecilia – in the more wealthy part. Doyle, on the other hand, came from a poorer area.

The character of the city was changing as it continued to develop, and there was now a 'New Town' as well as the original 'Old Town'. Over the last century factories and mills had been constructed, and workers had moved in faster than houses or water supplies or sewers could be built. They crowded into the old houses or into hastily built new ones. With no indoor toilets, they were forced to share outside 'privies' with many other working families.

The city had become known as 'Aulde Reakie' because it smelt so bad – in fact some travellers said it smelt worse than any city in Europe. Visitors inhaled the sharp vapours of rats' wee in Milne's Court and in the dark alleys leading off Leith Street; the semi-sweet odour wafting from the contents of chamber pots emptied out of windows along Princes Street; the intoxicating spirals of sulphur rising up from the locomotives at the Waverley Station; and the pungent stink of mouldy leaves from the gardens adjoining Queen Street. If they dared to venture beneath the North Bridge the air there was putrid with the stench of rotten fish. They found that the tavern yards whiffed of beer that had turned sour, and that the High Street stank to high heaven of horse dung. The basements and garret rooms and boarding houses, crammed with poor students and families who sold matches or pick-pocketed for a living, reeked of sewage and unwashed clothes. The fumes from the tanneries were so overpowering that families all around had to keep their windows permanently closed. Not least, there was the rancid stink of people's sweat – that of the lice-ridden stable-boy in Spittal Street, the janitor at the Infirmary, even Bell and Doyle themselves – though they smelled less of sweat, more of the Infirmary.

Such slum conditions provided the perfect breeding ground for the killer diseases of the day – cholera, typhoid, T.B. and diphtheria – against all of which doctors battled in vain. Bell had twice witnessed the dreaded cholera in Edinburgh – in the national epidemic years of 1848 and 1866. The disease was caught by drinking water contaminated with the sewage of cholera victims. Thousands of Edinburgh's inhabitants had died from it. Its symptoms were diarrhoea, sickness and spasms, followed by rapid dehydration and death. Sometimes he had known its victims die within twenty-four hours.

24

Typhoid also thrived in the city's overcrowded courtyards and underground cellars where the air was foul and where stagnant pools of household waste never dried up. Passed on through contaminated food, water and sewage, typhoid caused headaches, fever and diarrhoea. In Bell's day it was nicknamed 'the poor man's friend' because it cut down on the number of hungry mouths that a family had to feed.

The same was true of tuberculosis (or consumption) – another killer disease, spread in the tiny droplets of moisture produced when sneezing. Its victims could not stop coughing, and their spit was stained with blood.

But the children of Edinburgh were most at risk from catching diphtheria. With this disease, a thick grey membrane like a giant gooseberry skin would grow at the back of their throat and make them gasp for breath and suffocate. In 1864 when treating a little girl suffering from diphtheria Bell had performed a tracheotomy (incision into the windpipe). As there were no proper machines or instruments to help him, he had sucked out the poison with a pipette. But some of the foul substance had got into his mouth and he went on to develop a painful sore throat and found swallowing and speaking difficult. His legs became partly paralysed and it left him walking for the rest of his life with a jerky gait.

When Bell and Doyle walked into the fever ward of the Infirmary as colleagues in 1878, it would have ponged of foul breath and rotting flesh. In fact, during the summer months the air was so bad that some surgeons were convinced it was the cause of patients' deaths. Bell had plenty of horror stories to tell the young Doyle. When he started his career at the Infirmary, he had seen 'ward sponges' carried from bed to bed in basins, and nurses who had not bothered to change the water from one patient to another. As a result, many patients had caught hospital gangrene; their limbs would go black with infection and had to be amputated to prevent their whole body being infected.

By then his wife, Edith, had died of an infection

called peritonitis. Joseph and Edith had been very close to one another. They had been a devoted couple. His wife's death was such a devastating blow for Joseph that within three days his jet-black hair had turned iron-grey. Soon afterwards it became snowy white.

* * *

By the last quarter of the nineteenth century there had at least been one major improvement in hospital hygiene. Carbolic acid solution was being used as an antiseptic to drench every nook and cranny of patients' wounds to stop them becoming infected. But conditions were very far from being sterile. Many surgeons continued to operate in their outside clothes or in their favourite apron spattered with blood and pus from previous operations (their 'butcher's jacket' as it was known). No masks or gloves were worn, so they spluttered over the patient and passed on germs from their hair and fingernails. Some patients caught septicaemia during or after their operation. In his book *Notes on Surgery for Nurses*[*] Bell described it as 'a form of fever in which the blood and the patient are poisoned, as if by the bite of a venomous snake'. The patient's temperature rocketed, their pulse became weak, and coma and death followed so quickly 'that treatment seems vain and recovery hopeless.'

Bell was determined to improve conditions further – not just in hospitals but in the streets and in people's homes. He had worked out through logic and observation that the starting point was to try and *prevent* the diseases in the first place by better public health and hygiene. Every city had to be made clean and wholesome, 'sewage deodorized, drinking water purified and the air of every hospital ward made as sweet as the hills.' Students such as Conan Doyle would take these ideas forward in the years to come.

But treating diseases brought about by poor sanitation and hygiene was only one part of Bell's

[*]He also wrote a book called *Manual of Surgical Operations*.

work. He also had to tend to the gruesome injuries that any busy town of his day faced. There were 'doomed' legs that had been crushed under the wheels of a carriage and had become gangrenous; fingers that had been severed in a mill loom; burns from scalding vats in the brewery; and horrible deformities of the spine caused by carrying heavy loads since childhood. By the time that Conan Doyle saw them in the outpatients' department they would have been patched up. But his old teacher expected from him just as much attention to detail – especially watching for the slightest signs of infection.

Bell applied to his patients the calm and logical methods he had learnt from the ideas that had been passed down through the ages from Hippocrates. Diagnosis based on close observation. Attention to the little details, the 'trifles.' He had a very gentle bedside manner, and his soothing words of hope earned him the affectionate name 'Joe Bell.'

With children he had a particularly good relationship, both at the Infirmary and at the Royal

Hospital for Sick Children where he was also surgeon. Knowing only too well his own children's love of sweets, he even had a special box of chocolate pastilles for them. It was all part of his effort to understand and respect patients, and it was no more than what they deserved. As he explained in his *Notes on Surgery for Nurses*: 'You must remember that we, nurses and surgeons alike, are working on a complex, vital organism, not a mere mass of wood or iron.'

Chapter 4

When Bell was born, nursing did not exist as a profession. There was no training involved to become a nurse and many were totally incompetent. They would sleep instead of looking after their patients and would think nothing of letting a patient with an amputated leg get out of bed. The nurses gave them whisky and morphine whenever patients asked for them, and often drank gin and took opium themselves!

Meanwhile in London, at St Thomas's Hospital, Florence Nightingale was training a new breed of nurse. When Bell heard about what she had achieved he was deeply impressed. He, too, wanted to get a better class of women to train as nurses. And, at last, in 1868 he got permission to hold classes for trainee nurses at the Infirmary.

Three years later, when he was a fully qualified surgeon, he introduced the system of nursing from St Thomas's Hospital in London to the Edinburgh Infirmary. The training included visits around the wards with Bell on Sunday mornings and the nurses observed operations. They had to make sure that all the instruments were laid out on a tray ready for the surgeon and had been dipped in antiseptic solution so they were absolutely clean. It would be their job to see that the operating table was ready, that it had a waterproof sheet and dry warm blankets and pillows. The sponges had to be completely sterile, and if one fell onto the floor or into the box of sawdust (that was used for catching the blood) it had to be replaced immediately. As for the dressings, nothing must be left to chance. The nurse must have waiting everything a surgeon could possibly need. Finally, the bed had to be ready for the patient's return. There must be a waterproof sheet, a small pillow to lay under the stump in the case of an amputation, and hot water bottles. 'Have your hypodermic needle and the ether bottle ready... with beef tea, brandy and hot water... You will not have time to run for them when needed.' Good organization was the key to success, and one of Bell's favourite sayings was: 'a stitch in time saves nine.'

Some nurses were under the impression that they would be thrown in at the deep end. But their fears were groundless. As Bell explained, at first, probationer nurses would be expected to do very boring work such as washing up or 'cutting up some uninteresting old lady's dinner.' If they were lucky they might be asked to hold the basin of lotion in the operating theatre, or get a chance to watch a patient coming round from the anaesthetic. 'Never mind,' Bell told them, 'keep your eyes open and *your mouth shut,* and you will learn something.'

New recruits had to be serious about the job. The

Infirmary would not put up with what Bell called the 'lady craze for putting on a pretty uniform'. Any probationer who just wanted to 'play nurse' would get even less sympathy from him than the old 'drunken slob' nurses. Probationers had to have a commitment to their work (just as one might expect a clergyman to be devoted to the Church), and an eagerness to learn and to observe — take temperatures, keep charts, watch out for haemorrhages, and practise bandaging on dummies. At the end of their training, Bell's nurses would go out into the world properly educated and equipped. They would work sensible hours and care for their patients, so that 'no patient is neglected, the poorest tramp has a chance of recovery certainly as good as the richest peer [lord].' From the moment they set foot in the hospital, every nurse was expected to greet the patient and their relatives with a pleasant word and a warm smile. After all, they were entering dreaded hospital wards, perhaps for the first time in their lives, and were about to say goodbye to someone dear to them, possibly forever.

Being a true professional, a Bell-trained nurse should not gossip about patients. 'Above all,' he warned them, 'don't tell blood-curdling stories of operations if you have a nervous surgical case.' They must also respect what was precious to their patients: 'Don't hang an enema syringe [a syringe that is used to inject a substance into a patient's bottom] to dry over a crucifix.'

Some years later, Florence Nightingale wrote to the Edinburgh Infirmary Board of Managers to offer her congratulations to the nursing staff. She spoke of Dr Bell with the highest regard and thanked him for all he had done 'so wisely and so well' for the training of nurses.

* * *

In 1869 Edinburgh Medical School, that had become famous for anaesthetics and antiseptics, was just about to make history again. The Board of Managers informed Bell that seven women had been admitted to train as doctors. The agreement was that they were to be taught in separate classes to the men. Unlike some of the other lecturers, Bell accepted the women as students and taught them surgery, including the more gruesome parts that he taught the men. What's more, when they sat their exams at the end of the course, the women did well, some very well.

As the first women students finished their studies, Bell's own career was just about to take a new turn. Until now, his main energy had been devoted to demonstrating surgery and to training nurses. But his skills of observation and lightning powers of deduction had made him a well-known figure in Edinburgh - so much so that leading members of the city's police force had begun to take an interest in his methods of work. Forensic science, as we understand it, was unknown then, but Bell once again was pointing the way towards the future. He was about to emerge as one of the first medical detectives in the country.

Chapter 5

It was a winter evening 1878, almost dark outside. The last outpatient had left the Infirmary; there had been eighty of them that day. Bell and Doyle sat in the consulting room, Bell with his feet upon the writing bureau on which were stacked copies of a magazine for doctors called the *Edinburgh Medical Review*. Bell was the editor, which meant he was often busy late into the night checking to see whether articles were fit to publish.

The flame in the lamp above the bureau flickered and spluttered in its glass. It was the time of day when they would share a story. The surgeon stared across at his assistant, drew his hands together as if in prayer, and began:

'The day after New Year last, the maid who worked for the Chantrelle family at their house in George Street – a young girl called Mary Byrne – got up just before seven o'clock and went downstairs to light the kitchen fire and make her mistress a cup of tea. But before she reached the kitchen she heard from upstairs the sound of someone choking. She turned round and rushed back to Madame Chantrelle's room where she found her mistress lying in bed, very pale and with her eyelids closed. The girl shook her by the shoulder: "Madam, what's wrong?" she asked. "Can't you speak?" But Madame Chantrelle only moaned.

Immediately Mary summoned her master from his bedroom at the front of the house. He hurried to his wife's room. "I can smell gas!" he said as he entered. "Mary, open the window!" He went over to his wife and rubbed her hand. "Speak to me, Lizzie!" But there was no reply. She was already unconscious.

Chantrelle asked his son to run across to

Northumberland Street to fetch Dr Carmichael, the family doctor. When he arrived at about half past eight he, too, commented on the smell of gas in the room and told Chantrelle that his wife was probably suffering from gas-poisoning. So they moved her to the front room where the air was purer, then sent a message to the Infirmary asking me and Sir Henry Littlejohn to come immediately.

When we arrived on the scene at about half past nine Dr Carmichael was trying to give Madame Chantrelle artificial respiration and her husband was standing at the foot of the bed. He was almost hysterical. "Is it the gas again? I knew I should have done something about it. It's all my fault!"

Seeing as her condition had not improved by one o'clock, Littlejohn decided to order a carriage to take her to the Infirmary. That afternoon everything possible was done to save her but, sadly, at about four o'clock, she died without ever regaining consciousness.

Next day, the gas company sent one of their men

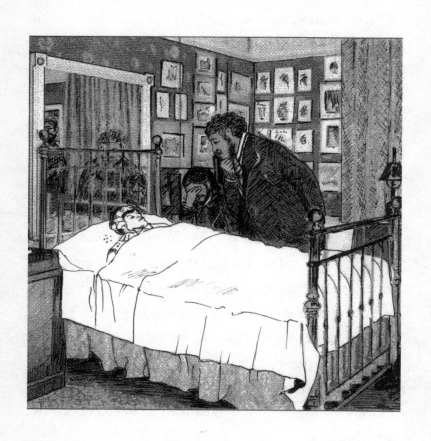

to the house and he found a broken gas-pipe outside Madame Chantrelle's bedroom.'

Bell looked down.

Had he finished? Doyle did not look very impressed by the tale.

Eventually he broke the silence. 'So, an open and shut case, Dr Bell.'

Bell leaned back in his chair, his long hands stretched out in front of him, his finger tips pressed together:

'That would be to ignore the little details on which cases like this so often rest.'

'But...'

'You know my method. Observe, observe, observe. As I have said before, it is the *little things*, the *trifles* that are so important. We all *saw* the scene in the bedroom. But did we all *observe* everything there was to see?'

Doyle looked puzzled.

'I happened to notice that on Madame Chantrelle's pillow there were a few tiny brownish spots and a few more on her nightgown. When I took the pillow and the nightgown to my laboratory to analyze them, I found that these spots contained tiny traces of grape-seed and opium.'

'You are not suggesting she was poisoned, are you?' Doyle looked sceptical.

Bell's keen grey eyes stared at his assistant. His expression was grim. 'That is *exactly* what I am suggesting.'

'But what about the loose gas-pipe?'

Bell turned away. He looked thoughtful. 'Yes. You are right. There had indeed been a problem with the gas. The gas fitter confirmed that he had fixed the pipe for Monsieur Chantrelle some months before. But, you see, there was no evidence of gas in Madame Chantrelle's lungs and none of the bright patches on her skin that you usually get with gas-poisoning. And then there is the maid. She saw Madame Chantrelle before anyone else but she did not mention a smell of gas at all. Doyle, remember to notice the things that *should* have been there but are not, as well as those that are only too easy to see.'

'But what about the gas pipe that the gas company said was broken?'

'What indeed!' smiled Bell, knowingly. 'Chantrelle probably ripped it loose himself.'

Doyle raised an eyebrow.

'You see, Monsieur Eugene Chantrelle was by no means the devoted, caring husband that he appeared to be.'

Bell opened the top drawer of the bureau and brought out a newspaper cutting. He handed it to Doyle who focused on a photograph of a suave looking man with sideburns and carrying a cane.

'Chantrelle was once highly thought of for his teaching at Newington Academy, and there is no denying that he was a talented linguist. As well as his native French, he could speak English, German, Latin and Greek. His wife, Elizabeth, was a former pupil of his. She was just seventeen, he was forty-three when they got married. Her mother had warned her against Chantrelle, and she was right. The moment they were married he thought nothing of going out with other women. He also drank heavily – a bottle of whisky a day. Parents soon heard about this and started to take their children away from the school. With fewer pupils to teach he had to take a cut in pay and this got him into debt.

His womanizing and drinking led to quarrel after quarrel with his wife. He was forever telling her to "go to Hell" or to "go and stay with your mother." Once he threatened "to make mincemeat" of her, and said he would shoot her, stab her or poison her in such a way that even the Edinburgh Medical School would not be able to detect what he had done. Another night, while drunk, he struck his wife on the jaw, pushed her out of the house and locked all the doors.

Two months before she died, Chantrelle insured her life against accidental death for £1,000. Then, a month before she died, he bought sixty grains of opium from Robertson the chemist. Sixty grains, Doyle, that's enough to take a human life.

Madame Chantrelle died on 2nd January. A few

days afterwards I accompanied two gas fitters to the house. We noticed that just outside her bedroom, behind a shutter, there was a gas-pipe that was broken, and that the break was fresh. Chantrelle claimed that he didn't even know of the existence of this pipe; then he said that his children had bent it by hanging their clothes over it. But it was only too clear from my own observations that the pipe had been broken by bending it back and forward deliberately and then ripping it loose.

I carried out a post-mortem examination but could find no evidence of gas poisoning. That did not surprise me. As I mentioned, I had detected opium in the vomit stains on Madame Chantrelle's nightdress and on her bed sheets. Her death was certainly not a simple case of gas poisoning, as she was obviously very ill beforehand.

Chantrelle put on a great public show of grief at his wife's funeral and even tried to fling himself into the grave. Those present who were aware of how he had treated his wife when she was alive were greatly surprised. And so was he, when immediately he returned home, he was arrested for her murder!

At his trial he had the nerve to say that, on the whole, their marriage had been happy. Although his wife had been extremely jealous of him speaking to other women and had threatened to commit suicide. But their little boy spoke up to tell the truth. He said how papa used to swear at mama and call her bad names – "bitch", "whore" and "slut"; how he used to hit her and make her cry. One of their many servants – not one stayed for more than a few months – said that Chantrelle had thrown a heavy candlestick at his wife and that it had hit her in the face.

At the end of four days the jury brought in a verdict of "Guilty as charged," that Chantrelle had deliberately poisoned his wife to claim the £1,000 life insurance money, that he needed the money to pay his bills. But right to the bitter end Chantrelle refused to admit his guilt.

When he was led to the scaffold in Calton prison, he was by all accounts immaculately dressed and seemed not at all concerned about his fate. Asked whether he had any last requests, he replied that he would like three bottles of champagne and an expensive cigar!

Chantrelle's last words from the gallows were "Bye-bye, Littlejohn. Don't forget to give my compliments to Joe Bell. You both did a good job in bringing me to the scaffold?'"

Bell smiled. 'You see, Doyle, how people will thank you for practising "the Method"'.

Chapter 6

After graduating from the Edinburgh Medical School Conan Doyle began work as a doctor in Plymouth, Devon. His teacher, Dr Bell, had prepared him well for his new job. He had helped improve his powers of observation and he could now make deductions about illnesses at lightning speed.

As a young, inexperienced doctor it took a while to build up his patient list, and for some months he had plenty of time to spare. In these quieter moments he managed to resume his interest in writing. Doyle had already written and sold adventure stories to magazines to pay his way as a student. Now he set to work on his first book.

Meanwhile, Bell remained in Edinburgh where his forensic work as a medical detective for the police force began to absorb more and more of his time. His abilities were so highly thought of that, in 1888, Scotland Yard in London consulted him during their hunt for the notorious killer, Jack the Ripper.

London at this time was a divided city. The West End was a wealthy area – full of elegant squares and crescents – where gentlemen would wear top hats and their ladies crinoline dresses. But the East End was much poorer with many slum districts and low-life criminals. For girls, there was little work available, apart from poorly paid domestic service, and there was no social security for those who were unemployed. Many girls became prostitutes in order to survive. Seven of these prostitutes who lived in Whitechapel, East London, were savagely murdered by Jack the Ripper between August and November 1888. Their deaths brought terror and hysteria to the area.

There have been many theories as to the identity of

Jack the Ripper, with one web site today giving twenty-one possible suspects! This is not surprising when we have as many different descriptions of the Ripper as there are witnesses to his crimes. Seen for the briefest of moments, one witness said that the attacker was twenty-five, another that he was over forty years old. One said he was only five feet five inches tall, another that he was a tall man of five feet eleven inches. One witness claimed he had a dark complexion, another that his complexion was fair. One commented on his dark beard, another said he was clean-shaven.

Witnesses found it all the more difficult to give accurate descriptions of the Ripper because the smoke and gas fumes of London created fogs. Known as 'Pea Soupers,' these fogs choked the streets so badly that at times you could not even see your own hand in front of your face.

In the absence of hard facts, rumours about the Ripper's identity were rife. It was widely known that the killer used a long, razor-sharp knife to slice up his victims. This led some people to believe that he was a butcher by trade, others that he was a carpenter or a shoemaker, still others that he was a barber, particularly as barbers at this time used sharp knives to lance boils and amputate limbs. Bell had read about all these possibilities in the Edinburgh newspapers, had thought long and hard about them but had eventually rejected them. The most important aspect of the case for him was how the organs of the victims – the liver, heart and kidneys – were always removed with amazing precision. This convinced him that the killer must be highly skilful in anatomy, probably a doctor.

The Ripper took great delight in taunting the police in a series of letters: 'My knife's so nice and sharp I want to get to work right away if I get a chance.' He also wished them good luck with their attempts to capture him. In one letter he signed off with a 'ha ha,' and in another 'Catch me when you can.'

Bell was fascinated by these letters which were published in the newspapers. In one, the Ripper

begins 'Dear Boss.' The expression is more American than English, suggesting that the writer may have spent some time in America. The same letter goes on to say 'I am down on whores and I shan't quit ripping them till I do get buckled.' This sentence was important for Bell: the Ripper seemed to have a grudge against prostitutes, perhaps he had had a bad experience with one.

All of the murders took place in a very small area of the East End and the murderer seemed to have the ability to escape into thin air, or at least into a murky fog. From this Bell deduced that the Ripper must know the alleyways and lanes very well, either living there himself or visiting them often.

As well as using logic to make deductions about the Ripper's trade and his motives for committing the murders, Bell used handwriting. He believed that by studying someone's handwriting you are able to deduce something about their personality. People had studied handwriting ever since the seventeenth century. Earlier in Bell's own century, the nineteenth,

Sir Walter Scott and the American short story writer Edgar Allan Poe became fascinated by what handwriting can reveal. They were Bell's favourite authors and he was well aware of what they had written. The study of handwriting had recently become a science and had been given its own name – graphology. By examining the size of the handwriting, the slope of letters, the up and down strokes and the pressure of the writing on the page, it was possible to deduce whether the writer was a man or a woman, whether they were old or young and how intelligent they were. Sir Walter Scott had claimed that if someone's handwriting was small and very neat they were well organized and honest – but without much sense of adventure!

The trouble was that the letters Jack the Ripper wrote to the police were all written in very different styles. Sometimes words were spelt correctly but at other times the spelling was atrocious. Take this one: 'Sir I send you half the Kidne I took from one woman prasarved it for you tother piece I fried and ate it was very nise I may send you the bloody knif that took it out if you only wate a whil longer...'

Sometimes the writing itself provided clues that an uneducated person had penned it – being large and clumsy with poorly formed letters. But, at other times it was copperplate, the immaculately neat writing of a clerk. The Ripper must be laying false clues to deliberately mislead the police.

From all this information, Bell and a journalist friend tried to deduce the identity of Jack the Ripper. Each wrote the murderer's name on a scrap of paper, put it in an envelope and then they exchanged envelopes. Both men are supposed to have come up with the same man. Bell published his findings in *The Scotsman* newspaper. Although he does not name the suspect, he does give a detailed profile. The killer, he believed, was a surgeon who had spent all his money on drink and women. At first his father had helped him by sending him cash but he started to squander it on prostitutes. One prostitute stole his case of surgical instruments, and since that time he had harboured a grudge against all prostitutes.

Bell notified Scotland Yard of his findings, giving the name of the man he believed to be the Ripper. The police gave careful consideration to Bell's views but it seems that there was insufficient evidence to justify an arrest. As a result, the name was never made public. To this day we still do not know the identity of the man that Bell named as Jack the Ripper.

Chapter 7

The last Ripper murder took place on 9th November 1888 when Mary Jane Kelly's mutilated body was found on the bed in her lodgings. By this time Sherlock Holmes had made his first appearance in print in Doyle's novel *A Study in Scarlet*. Little could its author have suspected that he had created a character that was to become the most famous detective of all time.

Holmes possessed many of Bell's physical characteristics: his sharp, piercing eyes, his hawk-like nose and his long, slender fingers – the fingers of a pianist. Doyle also endowed him with his teacher's lightning powers of observation, analysis and deduction. As he wrote in a letter to Bell: 'I have tried to build up a man who pushed the thing as far as it would go.'

From the very first few pages of *A Study in Scarlet*, Holmes is playing the same tricks on his friend Dr Watson that Bell had played on Doyle. The moment they are introduced to one another, before they decide to share rooms in Baker Street, Holmes says to Watson in a flash: 'You have been in Afghanistan, I perceive.' Watson is taken aback: 'How on earth did you know that?' 'Never mind,' replied Holmes, chuckling to himself. Watson was bewildered.

How had Holmes worked it out? He had done it so quickly. But there was a logical train of reasoning that ran: 'Here is a gentleman of a medical type, but with the air of a military man. Clearly an army doctor then. He has just come from the tropics, for his face is dark, and that is not the natural tint of his skin, for his wrists are fair. He has undergone hardship and sickness, as his haggard face says clearly. His left arm has been injured. He holds it in a stiff and unnatural manner. Where in the tropics could an English army doctor have seen much hardship and got his arm wounded? Clearly in Afghanistan.'

The Sherlock Holmes stories (there are fifty-six stories and four novels altogether) are packed with examples of the detective using Bell's methods. In a tale called *The Red-Headed League*, Holmes brilliantly sums up a client he had only just been introduced to by saying: 'Beyond the obvious facts that he has at some time done manual labour, that he takes snuff, that he is a Freemason, that he has been in China, and that he has done a considerable amount of writing lately, I can deduce nothing else.'

In another story called *The Crooked Man*, Holmes worked out that the thief must have rushed across the lawn 'for his toe marks were much deeper than his heels.' He always paid particular attention to 'little details' such as these, even down to the type of tobacco ash left at the scene of the crime – he had identified one hundred and forty types of ash!

THE LAST SOLUTION

HE FIVE ORANGE PIPS

he Hound of the Baskervilles
featuring Sherlock Holmes

HE SIGN OF FOUR.

THE RED-HEADED LEAGUE

THE VALLEY
OF FEAR

A STUDY IN SCARLET

But it might be the absence of 'little details' (Bell's 'trifles') that was the significant factor – just as Bell had realized that Madame Chantrelle's skin should have had bright blotches on it if she had died from gas-poisoning, but it did not. So, too, in the stories. In one, called *Silver Blaze*, an intruder has broken into a stable and stolen a horse. Holmes drew the attention of his colleague, Dr Watson, 'to the curious incident of the dog in the night-time.' Watson is puzzled: 'The dog did nothing in the night-time.' 'That was the curious incident,' replied the detective. From the fact that the dog did not bark he concluded that the dog knew the intruder.

All these deductions are made by Holmes in an off-hand, casual way, and once explained seem 'elementary' (he never actually said 'elementary, my dear Watson.') But to everyone else they seemed baffling because they had not paid enough attention to the little points that formed the basis of the deductions.

In the same way that Bell was interested in reading character through handwriting, and studied the handwriting of Jack the Ripper, Sherlock Holmes also analyzed the handwriting of his suspects. 'You may not be aware that the deduction of a man's age from his writing is one which has been brought to considerable accuracy by experts,' Holmes explains in *The Reigate Squires*. In *The Cardboard Box*, where two freshly severed human ears are posted to a distressed Susan Cushing, Holmes is busy once again analyzing the handwriting on the package: the writing is unclear; a broad pen has been used with very inferior ink. The writer, he deduces, must be uneducated.

Holmes worked with the police but, like Bell, had a poor impression of them. When Bell wrote: 'It would be a great thing if the police generally could be trained to observe more closely,' it could have been Sherlock Holmes speaking! Bell believed the police should examine the facts first and only then develop theories. Holmes' colleague, Dr Watson, was guilty of making the same mistakes as the police did. When Watson sees a mutilated body on the moor in *The Hound of the Baskervilles*, he is quick to identify it as that of Sir Henry Baskerville because of his clothing. But it turned out that the body was not that of Sir Henry at all, but an escaped convict wearing his lordship's clothing. If only he had observed first and not jumped to conclusions.

In Doyle's house in South Norwood, London, near where the Crystal Palace Football Club ground is situated today, a photograph of Bell had pride of place above the fire in the study. It was from this room where, in 1892, Doyle wrote Bell a letter acknowledging the debt to his tutor. 'It is most certainly to you that I owe Sherlock Holmes,' he wrote. 'I do not think that his analytical work is in the least an exaggeration of some effects which I have seen you produce in the out-patient ward.'

The following year Doyle's friend in Edinburgh, Robert Louis Stevenson (author of such books as *Treasure Island* and *Dr Jekyll and Mr Hyde*) wrote to him saying how much he had enjoyed the adventures of Sherlock Holmes. Only there was one thing that troubled him: 'can this be my old friend Joe Bell?' he asked.

Chapter 8

As each one of his Sherlock Holmes stories was published, Doyle sent a copy to Bell in Edinburgh. In doing so he took a risk. Normally, Bell loathed fiction and had been rude about Doyle's earlier stories because 'real life is so much more interesting.' But these detective stories were different; they intrigued Bell because they were full of observation and deduction. In fact, he was so drawn towards them that in 1892 he even agreed to write the introduction to a new edition of *A Study in Scarlet*. As he later explained in *Harper's Weekly* magazine, the story was a useful reminder to every reader that 'there may be much more in life if he keeps his eyes open.' The reader, too, could be like Holmes and make amazing deductions.

The adventures of Sherlock Holmes became more and more popular, the reading public could not get enough of them. So much so, that Doyle asked Bell whether he had any ideas for story lines. His old teacher had a busy schedule but agreed to put aside ten minutes each day to think up ideas. Sometimes Bell came up with something too complicated, as when he suggested a bacteriological murder more suitable for a modern spy movie. Nevertheless, Doyle managed to work Bell's Method into many of the Sherlock Holmes stories.

As Doyle became more and more famous, everyone was keen to know what had inspired him to create the character of Sherlock Holmes. And when a reporter from the *Strand* magazine interviewed Doyle at his home in South Norwood the trail immediately led to Edinburgh. Before the reporter could dash off a letter to Bell, Doyle sent one of his own, warning his old teacher that he was likely to be besieged by reporters and by 'lunatic letters' from readers who wanted his help to solve imaginary crimes. As it turned out, however, Bell did his best to answer the reporters' questions and at first he was happy to talk about his Method with them. Only through exceptionally good time management could he do this, for he had a huge workload. As well as his position at the Royal Hospital for Sick Children, Bell ran one of the largest medical practices in Edinburgh and made over twenty house calls a day. He continued his busy schedule even when his life was affected by personal tragedy with the loss of his son, Benjamin, from peritonitis in 1893 – the same disease that had killed his wife almost twenty years before.

For a while, Bell was intrigued by all the publicity and praise. He had been in the limelight before: Queen Victoria had paid him a visit at the Infirmary in 1881, and while she remained in Scotland he had acted as her personal physician. 'The dear old lady was so friendly, and I was not one bit flustered,' he wrote later. In 1897 the King of Siam had visited him at what had now become the 'Royal' Infirmary.

But these visits were different. They were to acknowledge work for which he was responsible, whereas he did not feel he deserved any recognition for Sherlock Holmes. With his usual modesty, he gave all the credit to Doyle. He praised him as 'a born story-teller' whose imaginative genius had enabled him to make 'a great deal out of very little.'

In 1894 Bell bought a house called 'Mauricewood' at Milton Bridge in the countryside, a few miles outside Edinburgh. Each summer it gave him an opportunity to retreat from the hurly-burly, not to mention the smells of 'Aulde Reakie'. It also gave him a break from the constant interruptions of reporters. At last he could work in peace in his laboratory with his chemicals, relax in the large garden and play with his young grandchildren. He loved animals and enjoyed studying the birds and walking with his dogs.

But he did not give up work. Far from it! Since the deaths of his wife and son he had flung himself into work with even more passion. When his friend, Mrs Jessie Saxby, once asked him what sort of life he preferred, Bell replied 'A busy one with a spring in it.' Should the idea of retiring or even taking a holiday cross his mind, he cast it aside. But soon he was admitting that he had 'worked too long and too much,' and he decided he must cut down for the sake of his health. First he resigned as editor of the *Edinburgh Medical Journal* and then, in 1897 the year of Queen Victoria's Diamond Jubilee, he resigned from his position as Chief Surgeon of the Royal Hospital for Sick Children. Florence Nightingale wrote a letter to say how sad she was to hear that he was retiring. But even then he did not fully retire as he continued as Consulting Surgeon and also gave his time freely at the Royal Hospital for Incurables.

Something he could not control, however, was the press: it never went away. By the time *The Hound of the Baskervilles* was published in 1902 Bell was being 'hounded' too – not just by the reporter from *Strand* magazine but by a stream of newspaper journalists.

Soon he began to miss the privacy he had valued so much.

However, his love of speed enabled him to escape their attentions at times. He bought one of the first motor cars in Edinburgh, hired a chauffeur and went for long drives. He never slowed down, he never tired of life. Above all, he encouraged others to practise his Method, telling his two daughters and grandchildren to 'use your eyes, use your eyes.'

When his health started to deteriorate in 1911, he still made his rounds in a carriage pulled by two bay horses, Major and Minor. To the end he would never charge his poor patients – neither the handyman's son nor the 'somewhat daft old lady' who wrote a poem praising him. He also continued to set aside one tenth of his income for charity, as he had done throughout his married life.

Bell died on 4th October 1911. It would have been his wife's birthday. He had felt her loss deeply and believed he would eventually be reunited with her. An appreciation of him in *The Times* the following

week marked the passing of a very special man 'of extraordinarily quick perception and deduction.' One of Bell's colleagues, Dr John Chiene, said that 'every child in Edinburgh is indebted to this great man.' His funeral was one of the largest there had ever been in the city. Hospital staff, surgeons, patients and the general public – all came to pay their last respects to dear old 'Joe Bell.'

* * *

Whereas few people have heard of Dr Joseph Bell, Sherlock Holmes is, of course, a world famous personality, and his address, 221B Baker Street, is one of the best known in the country.

Bell would doubtless be amazed at Sherlock Holmes' enduring popularity more than a century after his creation. He would also no doubt smile to think that he had a (small) part in it all. But he had never been flattered by the idea that Sherlock Holmes was simply a replica or clone of himself, as some readers may have thought. For, although they shared the same amazing powers of observation and deduction, Bell's personal habits were very different to the great detective's. Bell was not the incredibly untidy man that Holmes was. Bell did not keep his tobacco in a slipper and his cigars in the coal scuttle. Bell was not addicted to cocaine, did not practise firing air pistols indoors, and did not play a violin at strange hours of the day – and night!

When the press gave Bell the nickname of Sherlock Holmes he resented this. As he once said, 'I hope folk that know me see another and better side to me than what Doyle saw!' Really, Dr Joseph Bell deserves to be remembered in his own right for his many achievements – as a doctor, as a teacher and as a source of inspiration to all who knew him.

Key dates in the life of Dr Joseph Bell

1837   Born in Edinburgh

1854   Begins studying medicine at
              Edinburgh University

1864   Introduces tracheotomy for cases
              of diphtheria

              Bell catches diphtheria

1865   Marries Edith Murray

1866   Publishes his book *Manual of
              Surgical Operations*

1868   Begins classes for nurses at the Infirmary.

1869	Appointed Assistant Surgeon to the Infirmary
1871	Appointed full Surgeon to the Infirmary
1874	His wife dies
1877	Elected Fellow of the Royal College of Surgeons
1878	Chantrelle murder case Meets Arthur Conan Doyle
1880	Florence Nightingale thanks Bell for training nurses
1881	Queen Victoria visits the Infirmary. Bell is her personal surgeon while she is in Scotland
1887	Publishes his book *Notes on Surgery for Nurses*

Sherlock Holmes makes his first appearance in *A Study in Scarlet*

Bell retires from the Infirmary

Appointed Chief Surgeon at Royal Hospital for Sick Children and Consulting Surgeon at the Hospital for Incurables

1888   Consulted by Scotland Yard hunting Jack the Ripper

1892   Conan Doyle writes to Bell: "It is most certainly to you that I owe Sherlock Holmes."

1897   King of Siam visits surgical wards of the Royal Hospital for Sick Children. Bell resigns as Chief Surgeon at the RHSC but stays on as Consulting Surgeon

1911   Dies at Mauricewood, aged 74

Acknowledgements

Joseph Bell: An appreciation by an old friend by Jessie Saxby (1913)

Dr Joseph Bell, Model for Sherlock Holmes by Ely Liebow (1982)

BBC TV series *The Murder Rooms, the Dark Beginnings of Sherlock Holmes* (2000)